Call Centre Love Song

IAN GREGSON was born in Manchester and educated at Oxford and Hull. He has written for the *Los Angeles Times Book Review*, and published poems and reviews in the *London Review of Books*, the *TLS* and *Poetry Review*, amongst others. His critical books are *Contemporary Poetry and Postmodernism*; *The Male Image: Representations of Masculinity in Postwar Poetry* (both published by Macmillan); *Postmodern Literature* (Hodder Arnold, 2004) and *Character and Satire in Postwar Fiction* (Continuum: 2006). His current critical project is *The New Poetry In Wales* for the University of Wales Press, and that book will appear in 2007. He has lived most of his adult life in North Wales where he teaches in the English department at the university in Bangor.

Call Centre Love Song

IAN GREGSON

SALT

CAMBRIDGE

PUBLISHED BY SALT PUBLISHING
PO Box 937, Great Wilbraham, Cambridge PDO CB1 5JX United Kingdom

© Ian Gregson, 2006

First published 2006

Printed and bound in the United Kingdom by Lightning Source

Typeset in Swift 9.5 / 13

ISBN-10 1 84471 256 7 paperback
ISBN-13 978 1 84471 256 4 paperback

SP

1 3 5 7 9 8 6 4 2

for Ceri

Contents

Acknowledgments

Acknowledgments are due to the editors of the following magazines in which some of the following poems appeared: *The London Review of Books*, *The New Welsh Review*, *The North*, *Pearl* (Los Angeles), *Planet*, *Poetry L.A.*, *Poetry Review*, *Poetry Wales*, *Stand*, and *The Times Literary Supplement*.

The Personals

txt

since yr remve
i hav 2 send

u these
lke sand

letters the c
silences

lke i am def
wanting 2

sign in the dark
scrawl on yr hand

lke smthng
lost frm lve

Call Centre Love Song

I'm edgy now with looming blame.
To fall in love with just a voice!
You asked for me again by name
And boggled my poise like secret vice.

My office runs a strict regime.
Be *this* I'm told, and then I *am* it,
losing myself to please the team.
It's hectic at *Exotic Planet.*

We answer calls. The room is cramped —
too many screens like twitchy pools.
You talk as though you're free, exempt
from all restrictive rules.

I hate myself that I'm compliant:
Eight Reasons For Leaving Your Desk,
and none is loving a client.
You booked our *Scorching Arabesque:*

I pictured you riding a camel
piercing sandstorms in a blue burnous.
We've never met. It isn't normal
to feel your absence in my mouse:

it aches to call you up on screen
and give your name a cyber-face
and show me where and how you've been.
But nothing could erase

the gulf between us made of money.
You whisper your thousands in my ear
which stresses my lack of any,
and niggles my hope like sudden fear

and stiffens my finger on my mouse.
A hundred calls are stuck on hold
all listening to Johann Strauss.
I'm rigidly controlled

as though I'm trapped inside a screen
and made to picture all I'm told
and flicker with scene after scene
then empty like a pane gone cold

as the sun withdraws from its glass;
or like a mobile dropped in a squall
of voices in an underpass
that frailly repeats its lost call.

How I Invented Sex

Something beyond just planting seed,
something in a range of styles,
huge it was, this need.
More an explosion waiting, and our trials
revealed *Cool Sex* could spark it.
Huge it was, the gap in the market.

I spoke one morning to a guinea pig.
She'd waited for this forever:
like being suspended from a peg
and the wet ripples across her running all over
twisting inside out with the big
breeze that was flooding through her as she shook
in answer to the old need, and came unstuck,
hurtling away in the huge weather.

We could supply the lack
like the housewife wanted.
                         More,
our subjects fill up with fulfilment 'til they leak
out of themselves and out of before
into an after quiet, amazed, only slightly sore.

Thousands found themselves, through my technique,
reborn as virtuosi,
stars of erotic chic.
Others stayed beginners.
We needed losers as well as winners
who make it seem so easy
their feelings feel unique.

So quickly and so much!
And the climb so steep and so dizzy
I looked into myself like vertigo
and flared up like a match.

I cut a record, published a book
and hosted my weekly game show
Can't Fuck, Won't Fuck
to put more millions in the know
and get more millions to compete
and try to enter our élite...

I grew so big and armoured with control
and knowing fully how to be,
as though the world's a vast keyhole
and only I
could stroll towards it with the key.

That Change

The autumn afternoon he crawled about that damp pavement—
his second wife relives it now, as often before:

small stones that poked his knees and palms and briefly clung,
the not believing that change like from nowhere a slap—

the change that was taking hold as his lunch-hour lengthened
into hours where an urgent meeting should've been.

She can smell the exhaust where the dark tube breathed on him
and feel the grey-on-grey hard stipple of the paving,

see the mostly curving thin cracks in broken paving,
cracks *between* paving, grown with scuffed moss

at the furthest edge of his first marriage

where his tight routine slackened around his bar table
with its overflowing ashtray and turned-off mobile

and he was thinking of her, his second wife to be
who waits for him in the autumn evening four years later:

How many times must a man be made to realise
as then he must've done—as though he could feel for the first
     time

his ankles and knees, his palms and fingers—
what moves in him below his neck?

She can feel the traffic thrum in his fingers and knees,
in the subculture of dogs and ankles,

his second striped and longer tongue licking the cracks,
the gnarled and pitted kerbs, while voices and expressions

broke in waves above his head, dispersing
as he swam through the street towards their new life.

But all around her the darkness deepens and wonders:

Couldn't another change now start in him
out of her reach, so that his knees

fall to his knees, a change like an unsuspected place
surprising his fingers, boggling his eyes?

The Personals

I'll choose two people from this page—
one to want and one to be
all made up from those words, an age
and status, how to look and see
all unlike the who
I must be always being,
an I to fit a You—
send myself like a message:
cerebral but funny, leftish but skiing.

So many characters
in search of a plot,
so many futures waiting to happen
which to me will not—
cultured and wild, a Venus against furs:
such futures, on this page, open
where mine is married, mortgaged, shut—
to know who to want, and what *for*,
searching for Love, or nearest offer,

pose myself like a question
and watch the blond muscular answer—
tall and thirty, open to suggestion—
stroll towards my table
thinking *eco-anxious, sinuous dancer*
thinking *sporty, busty, fun,*
feeling a wish grow palpable,
doing all I've never done
and seeing the ghost of the possible

who slipped out of sight
where facing windows treble the light
and his figure that broke
and flickered—perfect match,
a partner bespoke:
nervous, unstable, bright
but lost by the bridge, the building-site,
park railings or subway, who glimpses catch
fitful as a shadow on a watch

but might be conjured by this spell:
my age and status, how I look and see—
but no.
I'll make these types my proxies,
make them meet like parts of me
where column inches lengthen and spill
knowing the pleasure of both sexes—
shrunk to a few words, then born anew
and stuffed through millions of letter boxes.

The Roof

A fortnight after my husband left for good
damp patches flowered on my bedroom wallpaper.

A handsome bald broad-shouldered man climbed from his van
and nodded at my roof: I needed urgent surgery.

A pretty boy, his son, with a nose-ring, and Bob
built to the sound of music scaffolding
like a skeleton worn fashionably on the outside.

Their DJ echoed from somewhere like a voice that slipped
inside me next to my thinking—also news, and sport.

Their hammers cut into the heavy slate
then deepened and undid the raftered skull

opening the soft pine until the splinters
showered through the skeleton and dust misted the windows.

Torn felt, long slats of furry wood with rusty nails,
broken slates and plaster heaped up in the garden from their dig:

my bed was empty but they were unearthing overhead
a lost storey of music and shouts and heavy steps,

my doors were open front and back to street noises
and they sang and danced around my kids on dusty boots.

The looks of passers-by all climbed the scaffolding
and entered where the secret was unfolding—

I minded at first the new exposure
then I didn't, and the next morning

rain was falling through me
but there were dry patches on the road under the cars

and humming hands cradled and rocked a skip
down to the road. Then overnight the street all joined

the purging with me: added to my soiled slate
a kettle, legless doll, damp shreds of thick wallpaper.

Someone to Watch Over You

Sometimes I think myself so near to you
almost you might feel my breath
stir your hair

hover and hover but never appear to you
like your lover after his death
lingering where

you speak to me but I can never reply
and yet I can never go
held by the force

sticking your face like a freeze-frame in my eye
pushing me to need to know
all that's yours

slipping that day through your kitchen window
stepping one trainer on your unit
jumping free

into your flat that says you need me to mind you
danger might surface any minute
telepathy

lets me feel your craving like a tune both of us hum
together though we're miles apart
absences

live in your bedroom like an arm that's grown numb
so the pumped-up luminous heart
yellow dress

single rose
I leave waiting to open
clues like *Killing Me Softly* sung on your ansaphone

mementoes
of something lying in wait to happen
where each detail of you would be thoroughly known

like a star
living for me in my cuttings
taped undressings shreds of clothing locks of hair

near but far
always please and scattered in things
and not fixed and nowhere at once and everywhere

A Foreign Body

Forces are secretly working
unknown to camera crews:
what flickers in my living-room
floats on the surface of news.

Insiders watch the forms all cloudy
blurred in the distance looming,
knowing already how they'll sharpen,
aiming their cameras and zooming.

But what the news had said was true
is over like a fiction:
all I had relied on growing up
like *mutually assured destruction.*

The changes happen behind my back,
I turn the corner shaken—
changed myself in secret but sure
the landscape is mistaken.

The forces in hiding will collide
and mix their DNA—
in Africa somewhere or the East—
and start to head this way.

I see a picture briefly, say,
from Russia: movement caught
in the corner of my sleepy eye—
some bar, some bank, some port.

This picture conspires with others,
forcing, by freak, a merger:
I'm not looking that way at all
and yet the picture's growing larger.

The foreign body I inhale
has travelled half the planet:
it's nothing to do with me
until I find I am it.

I step out of a future mirror
wondering what I want.
I walk towards me like a threat
and wear myself back to front.

My Husband is an Alien—

else why ignore the baby and me
up in his study or down in his shed
with the light all shrivelled from his face.
Like finding a different way to be
dictated by the spider in his head,
the old him gone and filled up with space—

at least since he lost his job.
Time stuns him and deepens like space
and he suffers the house like a shock
and lives all day at his club
and something else is looking through his face.
He's lost to himself like a sock

stretched out on a beach on its own
growing foreign to his own moods.
He's silent like listening in
to strangers plotting on the phone,
and walks his secret paths in the woods
forgetting how to be who he's been.

The day we watched the baby on the screen
floating in its monochrome
outlandish capsule, something got
into him, like fishing, golf—whatever would mean
(metal detection!) he'd be not at home,
but deep into headphones on his yacht

and the voices of weather and shipping,
all away from broody me who swells
and looks all day inside, inside
to where this force, not me, unzipping
my self, has planted something else
and where I grow so fully occupied—

while he's, in all the wrong ways, a new man
searching the suburbs for a new frontier,
and maps, statistics, like an alien spy
reporting what it is to be human
from the outside, like a pioneer
staring at patterns in the night sky

and itching to launch his pointy probe,
but also secretive and bound
tight inside himself where he's concealed
like condoms inside a globe:
deep into headphones hoovering a field,
listening for messages from underground.

A Professional Worrier
Official title: worry surrogate.

I noticed the Power first when Steve my best mate
was frantic his wife was playing away.
I worried for him—suffered all she might

be wanting, all the shaming why,
taxis and bewildered pavements, strange
landscapes lasting an hour

and living for them I began to change
shrivelling in the hands of my own Power
channelling the stress out of them into me

until they parted painlessly
and Stevie told the press
her secret changed in my fantasy,

how, lacking any, I had stole his stress
as though I'd worn his suit, her frock.

Then I was laughed at as a holy freak
but hired to worry for a billionaire,
divert his enervating ifs,

living the self he needed to ignore,
joining his nurses, minders, low-fat chefs.
I looked down dizzy from the peak of his rise

alarmed by his empire of sweets and cakes—
as though his body stretched its boundaries
I felt inside him how such bigness aches

that what was one is now so many,
speaking for him, acting his role.
All this was changeable as money,
edging always out of control.

When he was shot, instead of spare
parts I gave my whole self like a martyr:
we breathed together in intensive care,
wounds flowering in me like stigmata.

All the media wanted their share
and hundreds started to suffer
pain so big no body could contain
that burst from him and fell like rain
and when we started to recover
all proclaimed a miracle:
I hired the scapegoats who together
struck themselves down with the bleeding call.

My surrogates: each like a mother
lends their body to another

paying ourselves like a price
wearing like coins another's face
finding problems not our own

running on our skin like lice,
hearing in silence as though down the phone
blanketed by noise a slight cry

demanding our sacrifice

burning our skin as though the sun shone
solely on us through the hole in the sky

Hughes & Heaney & Sons

In poems by Hughes and Heaney, boys
are linked to bodies in the mud,
for Nature gives the male no choice
but do as he's told by his blood.

When Hughes is speaking through his hawk
he's really the man of his dreams—
as though the purest Will could talk
and stop him ripping at the seams.

When Heaney wants to dig with his pen
and verse to turn round like a plough,
his Earth is served by writing men
like a goddess from *The Golden Bough*.

Both Hughes and Heaney most lament
this goddess losing control:
a male cult taking over meant
a hardening of the male role—

and though they love this hardness too
they wish the Goddess would come back
to punish men for what men do
and give them all that makes them lack,

and punish men since punishment
reminds them of their mother's power
and how it taught them what it meant
to be a boy and lack that power

learning boys must grow up tougher,
thrilled and shaken that their drives
must make themselves and others suffer,
hurt and please them into lives
shaped as by a cruel lover.

Couvade

It takes some getting used to—men
envying women, feeling the moon

tugging at their tides, and then
the season shift in their blood and gut,

shrillness in their engine note, until
they sicken with the rougher ride,

belly like a nine-month binge,
tits a lazy lifetime.

The misfit foetus opens her eyes
uneasy, starting to suspect,

in the warm sleet of lard and lager
strap-hanging on a loose noose of gut—

where the walls squeeze
and the floor opens up—

like a refugee drifting
through a foreign crowd,

food pressing by her
pushed by the wrong contractions—

waking as though boxed in the dark,
to punch and scream at the coffin lid.

How Does It Feel?

(Lines On Tony Harrison's Gulf War poems)

He saw the photo on the Sunday,
started writing on the Monday

how the dead Iraqi spoke
like Palinurus or that bloke

in "Strange Meeting": you'll have read
before about the talking dead—

no problem then for this charred head,
except for how and what it said,

for when it leant into his mike
it sounded like a pissed-off tyke,

it sounded like his Loiner dad,
someone a world away from Baghdad,

his windscreen wiper like a biro
he's reaching for to sign a giro.

It seemed obsessed with sperm banking
and accused the yanks of wanking—

though spilling sperm's a minor guilt,
compared to all the blood they spilt

and this was just a metaphor
of the poet's you'll have read before:

The Waste Land and D.H. Lawrence
express symbolic abhorrence—

linking fruitless sexual practices
with decadence and cactuses;

they say we can't now ripen our oats
(this isn't literal—see the "Notes").

But notions so Weston sound all wrong
from that burned and foreign tongue,

whose last thoughts surely were a far cry
likewise from "epiphany"—

that writer reaching for his pen,
the cold coming and the three wise men.

And if you interview a charred head
("How does it feel, then, being dead?")

let him speak in his own voice,
not like a Yorkshireman or James Joyce.

That photograph and its violence
sit in an alien silence

where a fraught polyphony
might speak, but not epiphany—

transcendent insights that replace
missed moments of religious grace

are not just missing but unmissed
as a quill in a cindery fist

in that least meaningful of wars
made cozier by these metaphors.

Dead Eliot, Lawrence and James Joyce
could characterise a voice,

suggesting a sound reflective
of another's distinct perspective—

this was what was needed to suggest
the gulf between that head and the West:

how sounds happened in him—speech and song,
the foreign landscape of his tongue.

I'm English, and Wicked

I'm English in this Hollywood thriller
and it's not that I'm a killer
shocks you but the tilt of my jaw,
my snooty vowels and elegant suit,
this air that one was born above the law.
The crime I plotted in my Tuscan villa

involves a labyrinth of wire,
a map of the sewers and a worried timer.
I hold New York to complex ransom
while looking obnoxiously handsome
and torturing a social climber.
Centuries now, in a green shire,

my family's been the land it sat on,
and ships that carried cotton, slaves and tea.
The half-lit alleyways of history
echo and twist and lead to me.
But what went wrong was Eton,
perhaps, where I was buggered and beaten

so I'm not, you see, quite fully male.
My voice is pitched a little high
and that is why I'm bound to fail,
my bomb can't blow the big reactor.
Look at the shoulders on the good guy
who mumbles like a method actor,

this stubbly American pachyderm.
He won't be shaken from my trail.
He's driven. I'm the stubborn frontier
he'll push at like a pioneer
smelling of buffalo, leather and sperm,
the white symbolic whale

he's hot for and relies on
to put him to the troubling test
that stops him thinking and makes him act—
pretending one could push forever west
stirred up like a face some woman's smacked,
and wanting to stand on the watery horizon.

The Adman's Breakdown

My mind was deep in shoes
that 5 a.m. my dad had died.
I'd worked on how in shoes the tongue
is tied down tight: it could unloose
and speak—but now that went all wrong.
The shoes had let me down. They lied.

I grew up watching my dad's
ideas he'd talked about—between
my programs, clever, funny ads
where jolly brave homunculi
were fighting the kitchen clean.
He made the products hear and see

and entered their needy spirit,
their needing to be needed
that powered their sexy allure.
The teasing prospects that inspire it
made me say, one day, he traded
only tricks, he was a liar—

but after I grew excited
by what an ad-man can command:
I saw the screen grow sensitive
as though responding to my hand,
I felt my own desire requited
watching the products change, and live:

this sofa longs to feel
a body enter its embrace;
this car's familiar with a place
where mountains melt into an ocean,
clouds at dawn are parting to reveal
frustrations dispersing in constant motion—

until that 5 a.m.
when shoes were sticking out their tongues.
The things—I grew so scared of them,
their quiet voices, hidden thought.
Hoovers were humming manic songs.
And all the things dad bought,

I never believed as much in—
these appliances that learn to talk,
conspiring in the dark of the kitchen,
televisions that learn to walk:
the screen's big brain that springs to life
a fork that whispers, a smiling knife.

Boggart Holes

His parents whispered in the next room—
straining to hear was like this long
attempting to realise.
Numb shadows in the fog like constables
poke canes into the frosted tufts,
flowing smoothly as a punting flotilla
but raising the tips to their noses.
A deep perforation was widening
under his bed. He feared the falling backwards
into a darkness whose surface
the constables stir, from which the outcrops heaved
that experts dust for fossil prints.

He fears the darkness sifting underfoot
from holes, the boggart mouths,
their faces lined in staring eiderdown:
to be as lost as the armchair and the couch,
a lounge leaking foam into this rainy col,
eroding with their knowledge into waste.
So warned, his reconstructions are their motives
as identikits are faces;
as lights begin to simplify the valley,
delineate a town by numbers,
he animates the murderers, that pair,
like Mickie and Minnie slowed to jerking stills.

Writing in Milk

For the Greeks, the hidden life demanded invisible ink.
They wrote an ordinary letter and in between the lines set out
another letter, written in milk. The document looked innocent
enough until one who knew better sprinkled coal-dust over it.
                                          JEANNETTE WINTERSON

Chopping onions and hearing thunder
I cry because he *gives me the push*:
but if I wrote the words right, I wonder,
could I then get out from under,
rise above this crush?—

Cows might fly I think, but that's not right.
From German it's myself I translate—
in Wales and pregnant feeling I might
enter another state,
watching till I lose the blue kite

against the shimmering blue
thinking of white written on white,
of writing rising through
that waited out of sight
but how, from the kite's overview,

meadows shimmer and my outline dissolves.
My childhood places in the east
disguise themselves almost as themselves
but change their names. I flew the nest
and the struggle of the mismatched halves,

the awkward attempt at being one.
I'm foreign in this margin, and two—
jostling myself like a bad pun.
But look how my womb has its own view
of what's translated by the Spring sun:

enclosures warming towards flight,
the harbour brimming as my hand
closes on a pen. The kite
reads the dappled land
where leaves that waited out of sight

are suddenly written
around the cows in black and white.
Asleep I soar and swoop, fatten
like Dumbo and feel I might
glide above the stretched margins of Britain

out from under my crush.
And while I walk thinking of a word
so perfect so English that it's flesh,
out of the herd
a magpie rises like a Friesian wish.

Pagan Rob

The planet's now all tangled surface.
Rob can dig beneath
flight-paths and wires and infrastructure
finding a place original and pure
where he is the sky and I am the earth
or Spring requires my sacrifice.

In homage to my woman's power
he ties up my ankles and wrists
and gathers in our sacred grove
bluebells in an ancient shower
and strews them on my breasts and thighs
as though the world, from savage mists,
might rise again original and pure.

It rises from a stone-age grave
unearthing hints.
Its Life is there but *underneath*
and waiting like a buried spring—
jet beads, boars' tusks and *beavers' teeth*
we think on like a prayerful digging:
henges, chalk phalluses and *flints.*

We think we know from their remains
how pagans worshiped land and water,
felt in March the cold soil quiver.
Earth is dead, they must revive her,
truss a scapegoat for ritual torture
and kill her, crowned with daisy chains.

The victim shudders. It's arousing
how the Goddess is so cruel,
the hot demands of the horny god,
the pain that's needed for renewal.
We fathom that past like dowsing—
pagan ages surge through his rod.

He senses the pattern of *leys*
that join up places so the meanings meet.
He senses how the land lies,
the truth beneath the pavements, pasture, wheat.
These gardens are the Spring in disguise,
their heavy blossom's modern and too sweet.

What's sinful alters, and what's good.
I'm now the Goddess and my laughing mood
shifts to an icy one.
I grow compulsive and Dionysian:
bind his feet and then his hands
and then enforce my cruel demands.

Parys Mountain (1)

It was a lesson for my youth; sublime
in Burke's sense of terror enjoyed:
a scene John Martin might have painted
who combines Milton and mines.
For hell was everywhere underfoot.

Lowered into the gulf the poor souls
were weighed in corves; infernal heat
rising, and the spilt veins, inflamed the marl.
And later, when disused,—its sulphur and ghosts,
its fiery pitfalls under heather!

Too old for fell-walking I enjoy, now,
that soul-testing exercise across
an inward, torturous terrain.
The lake I lie on mingles umber and shades
burning with sunset and reflected copper.

On its surface I stretch my fingers
like a pauper's over cracks where mud
oozes through his cellar floor.
This is the great gulf inverted, with its souls
anatomised like Burked bodies—a glove,

emptied, pressing coins into a fob; a shoe,
disembodied, poised for blacking.
But the rocks that rain on me are nothing like
the crumbs I wouldn't share
that tumbled from my table.

Parys Mountain (2)

What worried us about the old workings
drew our kids who always returned
with war-painted knees. We set out now
in a red light, thinking of feathers
scattered along a sulphurous adit.

Cowboys and indians are staining the West.
A gorse bush bulges from a van frame
gagging its jaw-like hood: we strive towards
childhood and find the afterlife of ovens
and fridges, skeletal metals, badlands.

Slowly in the fire of pigments a rug
is being consumed to sparse sutures—
so we tread softly, treading
on nightmares and enjoying it like
our houses on fire, thinking of our wives

and our red hands and alert to smoke signals
feet might raise in the coppery dust, and ancient
childish voices that ascend the dark shafts.
The flayed open-cast reminds us of
wincing from touch. Our reasons for being here

are changing, or we enter a vacant place
between reasons, and although turning back
we meet our children half-way, we emerge
bunched for comfort like cars from fog,
in line and shining their cautious lights.

Phallic Shit

The damp of my mother's bed, the damp warm,
and the trail across her sheets

of her month-long lovers, summon
this slowest swarm

pushed out from the wet hill
through the cracks in our back door

to stretch out on the walls like an omen
in the morning in our kitchen.

I touch one
curled across the light switch,

one sizzles on a cooker-ring as it heats,
one cringes from my finger-nail

pushed into the tip of a rubber glove.
The kitchen feels them like an itch,

so featureless they're not a creature
but a blunt ooze

verging on nothing or water
and raw as a weeping sore,

each one a loose end
looking for something to love.

I salt them and they turn to semen,
but I'm guilty and identify

and think of secret pleasures
where my self dissolves,

and how they lose themselves
and blend

into nothing or nature,

how they're scared of salt the way a butterfly
is scared of scissors.

Freeze Frame

A household is threatened by forces that could open it up.
    A tannoy echoed in the living-room
Of a couple I knew, whose house looked down on trains and
    platforms.
    It unnerved me like a homely showroom,
Warm light on armchairs, serried lounges, all in a windy field.
    Perhaps the pressures rose then forced a change.
Lamplight had shone behind the curtains which embayed it like
    Their intimacy and the walls, but then
Maybe it had started to feel provisional —
    A shelter somehow not complete; rising,
Destinations prised a way through the furniture.
    Through a door left open I stumble
Detective-like into a frame isolated from a plot.
    On the table is a disappointed lead
Coiled towards its kettle, and leaves where he must have split
    The coupled tea bags. One of them had said
You're walling me in, for through a quarter circle
    Back and forward an erect umbrella rocks
On its pins, and I can hear two strangers in the bathroom —
    Conversation drifted there in the wind.
What ought to be inward was prised open, until they were
    Cohabiting with North Atlantic moods.
Their thoughts linger head-high above the pine-table, tangled
    As the flight-paths of a cloud of midges.
A cold front has spread from the kitchen. Causes tangle
    With symptoms; onions nude in vinegar
Jarred and smarting shudder on their old refrigerator
    That palpitates and wheezes, pumping its breath
Into a flat frozen in the puzzled look of a photograph
    Its subjects have vacated. Two stiffs

Are clasped together in the teapot like a couple in lava.
  Leavers and arrivers are embarrassed:
High above the platform the lit casement is uncurtained,
  Exposing its hurt interior to the dark.

A Coypu

Lovers between them can make
another mind whose ideas
neither apart would conceive
resembling *folie a deux*
as wishes resemble fears.

Lovers together even see
differently from each apart,
or so I thought after that walk
between the fenced-in marsh and the shore:
that creature hurried from you and me

down a line we wrote together—
neither of us could be sole author
both of its strong claws and its webbed feet.
Interacting we assembled
this tubby, furry other

pulling a tail like an afterthought.
I started as though from the danger
of what we'd make of one another
if my wishes conspired with yours.
The couple we are is a stranger

like the bright owl we must've made up
ghosting from the trees into a brief
tiff with a crow, then off through the park
a thousand miles south of its range
like stories we invent jointly that return
as memories, and haunt belief.

in the twin city

The Great Escape

After school he'll visit his grandfather
Who used to be a prisoner of war.
The people move so freely outside the home—
With wincing care, inside, and slow Zimmer frames.

Surely this can't hold his grandfather:
He'll escape his neighbour who complains
Someone's been digging her grave all night,
That her bifocals throw the ground into her eyes.

A prisoner of war like his grandfather
Can dig his way into the youthful streets.
So near he's come but his abandoned tunnels
Veered into sewers and electric cables:

Once you're under, sighs his grandfather,—
Ask the dead—it's hard to climb back up:
Often they find a gutter guarded by bars.
But always he finds his friends down there, his wife,

Mother and father, grandmothers and grandfathers,
And the colours of the waiting Spring.
He's looking forward to the past
His dig unearths like storeys under the floor:

The soil reaches out towards his grandfather,
Heaps of darkness growing under his bed,
The soil in daylight weights his holed pockets
But sprinkles from him, lightening his burden,

Preparing the release of his grandfather—
Downwards and then up. Out of biology
The escaping grandson gallops, frowning
At sunlight, clutching a sparkling Easter egg.

in the twin city

here are word pictures
they will help me learn the nice language
of the twin city

in the twin city
you are small and blonde but you are still you

in the stuffed subway the loathed bodies
also there I
grieve that you are lost

by the glass buildings the feared hollow
through the lost centre the desired buses

in the twin language
there are seven words which I can make
the required sentence

your surprised double
offers me a new beginning

near the warm harbour the entwined railways

I am sober or mislay the keys
to the red escort
take a safe taxi back that lost Friday

all the massed raindrops on the bright railings
hold the ghost centre but will break

by the glass buildings the repeat action
where I take my second chance
do not meet by chance that same Friday
your farouche sister

near the brick arches by the past river
mirrored by the massed windows

in the nice bedsit near the ghost harbour
on the same duvet
look it is beginning to recur

how the far mountains
are like hope and glassed
in the past river

through the glassed centre
number seven buses drive and do not stop
but will go on through the north suburbs
searching searching

Animations

I'd hardly thought of you at all
recently—it'd been so long, and how and where we lived
    differed so much. There'd been your call
it must be five years ago, you'd met by chance (and this revived
    a distance between us from when
we'd been close) an old girlfriend of mine, and I'd decided
    when we spoke again
I'd try to explain what happened, which was more than one-
    sided:
    but how could you see, being gay,
David, what I'd seen in her? Even with friends there's a gulf
    between us and the foreign way
they live—your business animation, and producing *Rolf
    Harris' Cartoon Time*, you'd fly
to eastern Europe and America to buy cartoons—
    but what you did would pass me by
like half a sentence heard by a driver as he tunes
    his radio and deciphers a sign,
except his destination and the broken clause
    mingle and so redefine
themselves and him, if slightly. So my life is swayed by yours
    as though by air apparently
still, yet infiltrating because in our formative years
    the gulf between you and me
was part of how I saw the adulthood we entered,
    silence, failure of affinity:
learning how for each the world is questionably centred.
    Now I'm husband, father of two
and the tadpoles are a virus under a microscope
    wriggling their tails, when I review

that day with Sue away: I cook, play, self-consciously cope,
    for the day in question changes
in the light of that evening, when a casual reference
    on television rearranges
March 21st from your perspective, and its severance.

    Quick shifts in points of view disrupt
expectations: upshots, downshots Chuck Jones used in *Bugs Bunny*—
    you enthused . . . Life's also abrupt,
I said: its camera shifts, its witty and unfunny
    angles show us up. And thought
how stills, spliced and multiplied, resemble movement as stories
    life, though slices, added up, distort
the felt continuities of self. My 80s worries
    were a caricature: you'd bought
a flat together, you and Ian, and must know the risks
    better than a straight like me, you two
metropolitan, street-smart, invulnerable as compact discs.

    I lived with my family and my view
of the mountains and the Menai Straits, and sometimes missed you
    recalling the naked rugby scrum
you fantasised about in Physics, or the fireman who kissed you
    in *Napoleon's*, but the sum
of all these slices won't add up to life: upstairs on a bus
    once, I said I wouldn't want to be
a father, and you said you would, some day you would. How does
    it happen? We, my children and me
set out to search for pondweed, worrying for our tadpoles
    without it; Paul stops for a pee

and wets his socks; we watch the lambs; I don't compare our
   roles,
      your tasteful, toy-uncluttered flat,
my semi: keep my temper, cook a pizza, kiss them better;
      Sue is back, it's 7 and we're sat
half-watching T.V. and I say I've taught Paul a letter,
      pressing *Play*, half-thinking that
Tracey Macleod is tremblingly beautiful, for I've recorded
      Late Again, and watch her eyes
follow her cue, which says Chuck Jones has been awarded
      the first David Platt memorial prize.

The Breakwater

Her drowned fingers brushed the breakwater—
This haunted the surveyor checking for damp:
He knew for all his fifty years the old woman
Who lived before her strange death in this house.
Widowed, she closed the seaview bedroom's door,
"For ever". As a child he passed the room,
Watching the sea swarm across its window,

Breaking across the shadowy bed.
Where wife and husband used to sleep
Was an absence like the nothing up a sleeve
Hanging flatly from a jacket.
Imagine a young couple in the bedroom
She abandoned to the sea noises, where she drowned
All their past! This haunted the surveyor:

She must have confused her husband with the sea—
Its brief identities shuffled together,
And vanishing. The room must have wavered in the bay,
A slow dissolve that read: Fifty Years Before.
The sea must have started where the landing ended
Though the house still felt the room
Like the ache in a severed arm.

Dream's boundaries vary like the tide,
Waking shores itself with crumbling walls.
She must have thought her husband had come back
When the waves cast their past on the landing
And she slipped into a sleep like an undertow,
Entering the surprising extension
With its snoring shingle and its drowned wall.

Why I'm Too Cowardly to Have a Vasectomy

Because I think I ought to understand what my *vas* is before they
    cut it out.

    ∽

Because I had a cyst cut out once from my lower lip and the
    nurse couldn't find the right scalpel

And the doctor said *You'd better go and look for it then* and settled
    back to wait

Except he had already cut the lip open and had to hold it shut

And I lay back looking at a strip-light and he described the path
    he was making in his garden, how he'd had to kill the
    weeds, then dig and dig and tamp and tamp then spread
    the gravel

And I replied with my eyebrows and tight noises in my throat

Imagining the nurse walking intricate corridors and climbing
    endless stairs, searching cupboards with infinite
    compartments

And she came back empty-handed and the doctor squeezed my
    lip tighter and said *We'll talk about this later—I'll have to use*
    this

And I never saw what "this" was.

    ∽

It's not because I think my life depends on my *vas*, or depends
       from it—

I've never been promiscuous and I've never been much good at
       fighting or drinking:

But we men are so confused now—we wouldn't know our *vas*
       from our elbow;

It's because I want to think of something secluded in me waiting
       for when I might need it, or not

And because I see my legs hoisted up gynaecologically—and
       think of what they do to women!—

And the doctor riffles deftly through his cutlery tray, and says
       Oh well, I'll have to use <u>this</u>.

Deconstructionists on Fast Forward

On Channel 4 the pundits find it
Terribly hard not drowning
But signing on the waves

Rippling across the screen;
They frisk an absent body,
Meaning slips through their fingers

Like bubbles from their mouths:
Faced with the failure of words
The deconstructionists

Throw up their hands
As though desiring words made flesh,
The dove descending—

Or a fantasy of the deaf
Seeing what they mean,
Bodies in the shape of a word:

Deft hands astonish deaf faces
And from their sleeves ideas
Emerge, unfolding their wings.

Shadowing

Who my employers are I've never known,
Nor what they have in mind for Marcus Ring.
The woman was persuasive on the phone,
Since then it's been all watching, shadowing—
We two like distant partners in a dance.
I've studied all the cuttings I was sent
Until his memories rise in me like my own:
Schooldays, Cambridge, marriage, high finance,
Then politics, the rise in Parliament.

I've watched him with his daughter and her soft toys
Sprawled on the carpet; also with a slow pen
Glinting towards me from his anglepoise;
And calming a farmer in a cold fen.
I've loitered, noting the particulars
Of meetings of the party, or committees—
Never with Russians, gangsters, hired girls or boys;
My forearms aching from binoculars,
I've watched his innocence in five cities.

Unless my stranger's vision is selective,
Making patterns in advance, forcing rhymes
With what's expected by a tired detective,
Partial because excluded, blind to crimes
Flagrant to insiders. If my own
Routine were watched, how would it look?
My neck stiffens with the strange perspective
Watching my back—the woman, say, on the phone.
My actions mistranslated in a notebook.

Snuffed candles, bitten apple, smiling face—
Mere freaks of my attention linger,
Impasses, not clues to his disgrace.
That farmer bridles; where he points his finger
Broadens and dissolves into the coming night:
I'm tired of the vain hope for scandal,
My sense of purpose bewildered in such space.
His wife, one evening, switches off the light
And then is lighting candle after candle,

And they close their eyes, I think—I strain to see.
They fall on all fours. He crawls around the couch,
She frisks the walls. Is this a parody
Of my blindness—how they move by touch?
I shrink into my shell as they collide
Hair, mouths and throats, and vanish in a grapple.
Later, near Ely, I hunker in a tree,
Darkly, in his garden, envying his side—
His daughter's playmate drops a bitten apple,

Boy and girl both naked. But how far from grace
I've fallen, and from who I used to be!
The mirror shocks me with my own face,
Now it belongs to someone not quite me
Whose wife and daughter left him from neglect,
Who follows on a lead—who has no choice,
Whose world is nothing but the case.
I've followed Ring so long that I affect
His pensive gestures, languid posture, stage voice:

I think it's me sometimes in committee—
I deploy all the details, they're impressed,
I'm going to transform the inner city.
Then they're shocked: I'm wearing just an oil-streaked vest,
I falter, digress—my breached defences
Threaten theirs . . . Yet powerful hands, in secret, tie
We two into a fraught complicity:
He glanced up right into my lenses
Once, and smiled, as though I were his alibi,

As though he likes to lead me in a dance,
Courting this private (like the public) eye,
Forcing on me strict patterns in advance,
Knowing that I've grown to need them, to rely
Even on the sad hope for scandals,
That I fear most feeling lost, as when that fen
Bewildered the thin spoor with distance:
Bright narcissi in a breeze, like candles,
Guttered and left me in the dark again.

I need imposed on me a cramped space
Of self—strong hands to lead my steps, a set
Course, the will of others, and to know my place:
My course would open like a road-map, that net
Of choices, and devour me if I were dismissed,
Or scatter me into nothing and nowhere—
A cringing blur out of my carapace,
Or taut balloon drifting from a tight first,
A tiny stretch at risk from too much air.

Thomas the Tank Engine Reaches Puberty

Thomas thought he was a train—
Pistoned his arms and chanted *choo-choo*,
Gathered speed and said as he ran
I think I am I think I am I think I am

He woke out of a restless dream
And found his blood was steam
His face a silver disc
His voice the many wheels
That said as they ran
I think I am I think I am I think I am

Could he be an engine?
All his friends boy-engines too?
No mummies and
No daddies and
No teachers?
All day chanting *choo-choo-choo*?
Wanted to stop this thinking
And to say as he ran
I think I am I think I am I think I am

Then he noticed girls
Who had wheels and windows
Corridors and comfy seats
Were helpless carriages,
Were lacking steam and pistons,
Needed Thomas or another engine—
Needed marriages—
Even to say as they ran
I think I am I think I am I think I am

But then he noticed also
All the world was a shallow sham —
The country where the rails ran
A mere facade for miles and miles,
Merely puppets all the people —
Stiff their postures, forced their smiles.
Surely Thomas must be real —
His wheels worried as they ran:
I think I am I think I am I think I am

He grew and grew and grew
Obsessed with tunnels and with couplings —
And his steam sang *choo-choo-choo*
And his steam surged inside him
And he charged along the track,
Hurtled off the rails
And landed on his back.
The moon looked down on a silver disc
Frowning like a boy's face,
Glinted on the slowing wheels
That could no longer
Say as they ran
I think I am I think I am I think I am

Thomas was sick for weeks and weeks
Being mended in the works
And when he was as good as new
Worried he was not the same choo-choo
Because he had such different parts:
Said, "Am I Thomas now or who?
I'm Thomas and not you or you"
And his new wheels said as they ran
I think I am I think I am I think I am

The Hawk at the Shrink

Imagine, said his analyst,
A salt marsh.

Behind his shut lids
The darkness persisted,
And persisted.

Then he saw an old wall,
Weathered from without
And eaten from within;
Unyielding, standing up
Against the salt wind.
For long service, this wall's
Decorated with lichens.

No, his analyst said,
Imagine a salt marsh.

The land he can grasp,
The sea imagine.
But their mingling—
Like water and air,
A grey day—
The frosty weather he prefers,
Its hard clear light
Affirms each object—
Separate, itself.

His analyst was firm.
She said: *Together,*
Sea and land.

There followed an expensive silence.

Then, dismayed:
Receded tide,
Slovenly foreshore;
Slack meander where
The spineless river
Loses itself.
Small heaps of
Soft phalluses,
A thousand bubbles
Bursting under mud—
Shrill murmur of
Feminine victory.

The land and water
He mistrusts; but he admires
Fire, which is itself,
Or nothing.

Voice Over

Your closest ally in your government
Leans on two surprised words till they dissent
From themselves, and stumble into menace.
Others conspire to threaten sentences.
Doubt loiters with Intent, Defy with Die:
You fly, drive and drive and hole up in Venice.

You'd feel at home in the quatrocento,
You're not a tourist puzzling this memento
Of fear and glory, needing to ignore one
To feel the other—brilliant propaganda,
Stolen saint and bronze horses and thunder,—
Falling between two minds in oxymoron.

The Doge's Palace has division in-built,
Contrary chambers, wide and narrow; secret guilt:
Inside the sculptured head of this lion
The throat's a box for delations; a tiny keyhole
Turns this wall into a door, which turns
Gilt and marble into stone and iron.

You think of the arsenal and the ghetto
As you walk recesses Tintoretto
Has not endorsed with triumph or allegory:
Those legacies and this—to be removed
Down corridors, across a bridge, past a hateful
Glimpse of San Giorgio Maggiore.

A tiny key can turn inside a word,
Reversing all to which it had referred,
Startling at its back the resonance
Of bare chambers, echoing stone stairs,
And oubliettes of voices in your country.
Fear made Venice threaten, pray and think askance—

It built a castle to defend its wealth,
Churches to petition God for health—
On threatened foundations, wary premises—
Feared Hell, high water and Black Death; but throve:
So made this Palace from the castle;
Suffered, though not that last nemesis

Of flood and plague. But in a state of fear
Some words dissemble, others disappear
And leave you acting out a baffled mime
Voiced over in a language not your own.
Ghost-written others echo at the mikes;
Encode and hint, divide or quietly rhyme.

Elusive Boy

It's mum. That's posh now, this machine—
It's like you though, you were always clever:
"I'm out right now, but speak after the tone."
But what I wanted was to thank you, Dean,
For the car, and also Trevor
Wants to thank you, but won't phone.
We've washed the tyres and hid the spade and fork—

We love the car, don't get me wrong,
Though Trevor says it's been through hell.
He's saying you and him should talk—
That "model" and that queer, you don't belong
With them. But Dean, please, give me a bell.

~

It's Jane. I've been to the flat four times.
You didn't say you were going.
Like a fool I tidied the place up.
I know about your little crimes,
Remember—your toing and froing
And wheeling and dealing.
                              Face up
To us—apart from me there's no-one
To care about the Dean you bury
Under all that con and pose.
Your friends have nothing to go on.

Why leave in such a hurry
You scatter the floor with clothes
As though the real you and your disguises
Are tangled in a fight? . . .

It always stirs me, mind, imagining
Several of you (though in the same sizes)
Helping me make it through the night.
Soon as you get back, give me a ring.

~

Jeff here . . . Who's an elusive boy?
You're badly missed by my better half
Who made up my mind to phone you.
Why did you get so troubled and coy?

You're more than just a member of staff,
And ever since we've known you,
You've used yourself, you were your own ploy
And dressed up for a laugh,
And no-one said we own you,
So why should you disappear?
Unless to "find yourself"
(Though what you find won't be you at all).
Unless it was out of fear
Of how you've redefined yourself.
Come back soon and give us a call.

~

It's Trevor. Oh, you'd be in stitches —
But I do feel your thoughts, your mindset —
Though you'd listen to your own twin
Less than those telephone bitches
Rubbing their clothes against the handset.
Open your lines, please. Let me tune in.

～

It's Jane. Don't leave me this way.
I ought to kick you. Once I fought a
War to get clean, then felt I'd fallen
Flat into a straight day.

The world has turned to water,
I'm a tea bag leaking and all swollen.
Once I reached my hand out in the night
And touched, not you, but the edge of a trench
Which crumbled. It was for a drain.
The steps led down a flight,
But there were clothes rotting. And the stench!
Come back. I get no kick from cocaine.

～

It's Trevor. Somehow you're gone now
More than before, when I have flowed
Out blindly to reach you along
The streets of thought. I'm down to one now
And need to speak to lift this load
Off my chest, and the crumbs of soil of my tongue.

～

Jeff here. Call if you're around, I'm worried.
You're lost wherever you are—
You'll be wearing the colours of that place.
How many of you have you buried?
After we'd pushed through a crowd, once, you wore
Somebody else's face.

You've grown up to be multi-storied
But I still think of the boy you were,
A glue-sniffing naif and hard case,
Dying to be someone, and becoming
Three initials on a Jag's plates,
Endless changes of clothes,
And now this dumb phone—you're all-consuming . . .

Like a fire underground that depletes
Itself, and hollows out the more it grows.

~

It's me. I don't know why you went.
Now I have to talk to this hissing
Of distance, this hissing of no-one there:
Though talk was a dead letter sent
To you always, to somebody missing,
Or never how they seem, pointless as prayer.

Fast Asleep

The driver fell asleep at the wheel
as though the edge where she'd been pushed
crumbled and she fell, but floated
and the car continued regardless
with its windscreen like a TV
turbid with disputing heads—
the merger had pushed her to the edge
and they were shouting it was wrong, wrong!—
her cigarette was burning
fifty seconds from her fingers
but her wheels were inching to the left
as the motorway was sloping
under the light rain and flashes of sun
down towards the sunlit city
where the river broadened,
all before her shut eyes
so when she looked into the windscreen
she saw her husband smile and
whisper in that woman's ear
as she careered below a kestrel
that dipped, then rose, then hovered
like a moment of stuck time

Fast Asleep Too

The driver fell asleep at the wheel:
his colleagues always admired
the way, with setbacks, he could
continue regardless—not knowing
he was knotted hard like a golfer
locked up tight into his backswing
and forbidden to unwind—
but now his hands softened, and his head
slackened—just in the middle
of everything, the long dispute
with his father, and the lack
of closure with his wife—
his wipers can't erase
these pictures in his windscreen,
and he's a thread pulling loose
in the middle of the network—
direction signs that stare at him,
the slip road not taken,
and the haven of the service station,
headlights in his mirrors
igniting through the rain—
but the middle lane's like home to him
and shelters him for miles:
as though he could continue asleep
into the city and his parking-space,
sleepwalk into the purposeful lobby,
then hum in the lift to the fifteenth floor,
and his screen that welcomes him by name.

Carriers of the End

"... I mean such as had received the contagion, and had it really upon them,
and in thir blood, yet did not show the consequences ... These were the
dangerous people;"

(DANIEL DEFOE, A Journal of the Plague Year)

"Once, when a whore accosted me, I bowed, 'I deeply regret it, Madam, but I
have a friend.' Once I carved on a seat in the park, 'We have sat here. You'd
better not.'"

(W. H. AUDEN, Letter to a Wound)

The enemy Defoe identified
Were limpers, wore white caps and scarves tied
Around their necks; the looks of others lied,
Resembled ours four hours before they died.

They've stood in moonlit forests side by side —
The pastor and polluted wretches — cried
To the devil, watched the witches ride
On the air. In daylight they subvert us undescried.

They saucered here because their planet died.
They hate our values but they hide
In human form, except they're laser-eyed,
Their feet are webbed. They're plants inside.

They're really reptiles but they've occupied
Your boss, your daughter — live because they died.

They've chronic wounds they've closeted inside
Their normal clothes; in letters they confide:
"I love you, wound. Please be my bride."

The wounds are quiet, or they've lied,
And spawned in other hosts, and multiplied.

Following the Charts

The secrets of the X-ray and the tests his wife
wouldn't guess, he seemed the same, and he confided
only with his boat, which looked at him askance.
His wife was jealous of *Rebecca*, said it widowed her—
and often that unsettled autumn he slept below her deck
preferring to his wife the boatyard's sisterhood,
their naked halyards screaming in the wind, stuck fast
like an envelope in a blustery hedge.
He caulked *Rebecca*'s wooden splits and fissures,
healed her paintwork: dying is easier like this,
turned into a destination to arrive at,
stocking up the fridge, remembering the flares
and life jackets that make him suddenly smile.
He carries around the doctor's forecast
like cargo in his hold, together with a colour
like tiger lilies, the hinted lure of what is far off
trapped amongst the boatyard's ragwort, and uncanny growth,
knowledge he should've happened on before

this morning in Spring: the hoisted sails, *Rebecca*
looking at him askance again because he thinks
that she's the answer, and this late beginning where water
swells and deepens—but the currents are charted—and the heat builds.

The Creature from the Black Lagoon (U.S. 1952)

Monsters are attracted to women —
I mean those 50s man-made figments in films.
The men can't understand the woman,
The lagoon, the gentle monster, because they're like
Water-skiers skimming the deep's surface
Elegantly; when the webbed, hairy claw is thrust
Into the port-hole they recognise it
Like someone alone with 'flu discovering
The distances, the bad climate
In his house — their premises grow strange as though
A river were running under them.

The gillman is half man, half fish and half fear, half wish;
The woman, in her 50s way,
Invites him — she's always undressing, always
Standing to one side of the group
Flirting with the night, like children in a tent
Sleeping in the garden, who want
The front door left ajar. So, now, their threshold darkens:
The leading man is dozing,
The woman is changing her clothes again, the gillman
Rises from his spacious ulterior —
But only to have a look. The men are business men,
Though, and scientists; these frogmen must
Follow the monster under the water and above
Into its dripping labyrinth —
They've come to catch a wish for their aquarium.
Instead they find they've poisoned the fish,
Which lie limp on the surface looking sideways at them.
Their confidence is shaken, like that

Of a water-skier glimpsing all he's standing on;
      They've angered the monster, they must escape.
A grasping desire has exiled them from the lagoon
      Making them feel in their own element
Like fish out of water. And when the film ends, I'm like
      A frogman waiting to rise,
Treading water just below the surface, learning
      To breathe again at a lower pressure.

Vengeance is Mine

The two were perfect friends,
Except they judged each other
Harshly over tidiness.
Only death would part them—
One was Catholic,
The other Anglican.

Sooner than they thought
They parted: from her window
The Anglican watches
Trying to imagine
What Hell means to her friend, this Hell
Lying about her in her old age.

Since tidiness obsesses her
She must employ her walking-stick,
Eternally, to clear leaves
And litter from the street
Which grows fraught with meaning
Like a poem by God:

Its wicked never rest,
Its proud continually fall.
The author of her suffering
Shakes the autumn through downpours
At her hesitating feet;
The leaves are carried like lost souls
Forward and back in the wind.

Whose vengeance is this?

Sighs and lamentations
Swell from the railway-line,
The next circle; for the souls
Shrieking in the playground
Third childhoods last the longest—
Spinning and swinging
And jerking up and down.

Poor dear, she peers up
Through her thick glasses
And can't remember where she is.

The Vicar and the Rag and Bone Man

He looks and beholds a pale horse
trotting past the consecrated ground
that rises from his half-demolished parish.

Brick dust and splinters fly in the faces
of four angels—air and vacancy
church light irradiates into form—

who, higher than the half-completed flats,
survey interiors wet with rain,
staircases climbing to the open.

At corners the rag and bone man rides
into vacated feelings, and reoccupies them.
Legs and arms tangle on his cart.

His rags remember bones, shaped to their contours;
crumbs of skin cling to their clothes; a mirror,
broken, hatches dead faces in glass.

The angels sound their trumpets
above these revelations,
and predatory hearses circle the estate.

Happy the Man

A general in my pensive retreat,
Self-exiled from all parties and sects,
In my own ground I wrought the sacred cause
Higher into the gardener's effects.

And so God's seasons, like my moods,
Were glassed in all that we had made
Until the lichens started, suddenly,
Shrivelling on the colonnade.

The glass held only me—until I was,
Not banished from the garden, but joined there:
Benches on my seat, and thoughts of others
Rippling my standing pool of air.

Glittering in the chandeliers, hazy
In the billiard room's southward view,
Manchester was looming, more substantial
Than my scagliola and ormolu.

The terrace flickered with interference,
With man-made fibres walking mongrels, ghosts
Washed up from a council estate, from air
Stirred into waves by wires and masts

—Which lifted reflections from those waves
And lined the clouds, showering traces
Not of God, across the park, but voices,
And a snow of faces melting on the leaves.

The Sick Room

A Dislocation

When I was five and my father died
I started to stutter.

Where we lived when I was five
is difficult—

a stretch of carpet leading to a door.
It struggles just to *be* a place,

no ceiling and no walls,
no storeys above or underneath

like words that shut themselves tight
away from me—

no sister and no baby brother,
floral carpet hovering and fading,

and my mother off to one side,
and hardly even me

who's five now,
where words are difficult to climb.

The Sick Room

A man reading *The Daily Herald*,
A woman and her pram, struggling with a bag,
a girl skipping and talking to her doll,
two workmen running in overalls —
my father jerked his hand up pushing them away
as they passed through the curtains and door over his bed.
I was five. My mother wouldn't let me see how hard
the room was taking it. It wasted away,
worn to nothing by pedestrians filing through.
Colour was draining from the roses on the wall.
The ceiling thinned, letting in the sky.
Tarmac was emerging through the floor.
My father whitened, turning into his sheets.
One morning there were street noises behind the door.
The city repossessed the room, swept the curtains back.
Distances entered. Last time I went there,
the room had been worn to a pavement by the feet.

In the New House

I never thought of how it felt to her.

My mother had a stroke—
one arm was dead, one leg in a caliper.

And all the words she ever spoke
fell on the floor and broke.

Five months she was away.
I went to school and out to play,

and by the time that she came back
she leant to one side and was slack.

My stutter joined with hers
so when we spoke

our words lay broken all over the house.

A Dental Appointment

The old kitchen, just before:
her arms heaped with washing, mouth gagged with pegs.
The walls sloughed and grew two skins,
cupboards fattened, smelling of paint,
the table lengthened and shone.

I'd hurried home, was missing my appointment,
while she was lying on the couch.
Twelve neighbours were pronouncing,
superstitiously, upon the danger,
when combined, of washing-day and dentistry.

My jagged tooth had done it.
Her right side was softening
into a mist I parted: the arm
was deadened, and the leg calipered.
And all the peggies on the carpet!

The couch was growing into the suite
it would be after she returned.
Her mouth fell open: all her conversations
chattered out high-pitched, rewinding;
her sentences were scrambled after.

Ambulance men removed the old furniture,
the pegs were broken on the stone floor.
My tongue tested the half-gap of the snag,
my roots aching over older incisors;
removal men stretchered her away.

Her Mother's Way

And while my mother was away
her mother came and took control,
and after felt she had to stay
as though my mother must replay
all of her childhood trying to be whole.

My mother now was *Jean*.
Our house was altered to her mother's way,
her loud stilettos and her knitting machine,
the pullover that chatters and unfurls,
the secret pocket sweetened with eclairs,
the miniature poodle and the soft grey curls,
the wool-balls jumping where she sat.

And then my mother never dares
to sit around with friends and smoke
but being again her mother's daughter
must be punished for her stroke
and learn again to walk and talk
watched by the woman who first taught her.

And my mother lived twelve years like that.

From Whose Bourn

My mother had a stroke, and you,
Her mother, came to take her place—
Continued when she died.

This wintry photo of you
And the beach at Newborough Warren
That day in summer, they're combined now:

For in the photo your hand
Shades your cataracts as though
Peering after me a beach away.

That day the summer was uncertain
Like a memory; I walked
Miles to find the sea, and you,

Behind me, were a wave growing smaller.
Two yachts, the shore apart,
Placed the sea between quotation marks.

I drove to Newborough again today—
A day in winter uncertain
Like a memory, as though

Two pages had turned forward at once
Into summer, or as though summer's
Writing showed through under winter's:

A flock of birds like a heat-haze
On the flickering horizon, a cloud of midges,
Bright deceptive sun and warmth like a reprieve

Except for the ice
Stretching the shore's length in a frozen bourn
Wide as a single-track road,

The warm spell suggesting a return
Except for the ice-road,
The one-way traffic of the dead.

A year ago I raised my voice—
Poor hearing made you seem far off.
And through the camera lens

You were already small. I think, though,
Maybe we were never close enough, as now
You're peering from the cold snap in my hand.

The Smaller Picture

I'd hate to go back there —
cramped space of childhood,
square mile, the small house and school,
cramped space of knowing
bounded as though a fence
surrounds it all, and I must grow
to see above it: smallness
ties me to the ground, I can't
remember there being a sky:
grain of paving, carpet pattern,
tarred stones of the road, the grids,
council estate with fields behind,
grey grass, and bushes with thorns
and red berries I couldn't name —
I knew I was a boy, but not
what class we were, or how
my family fitted with others,
like a map pushed up
close against my eyes,
no sense of where the streets might lead
to others, and the cars to roads
and places the TV harbours —

and if I wanted to return
to feeling like that
I'd stare closely at the ground:
grass blade, dog turd, millipede.

Superman and Lois

Superman

I grow so hard
switched on by a night frosty and starred

my hard-on hauls me across the sky

I gaze out through the window of my hard-on
gasping I'm so high
and push on deeper and burst the sky

and hurtle light years into the night
hauled by the burning engines of my hard-on
gripping its tow-bar grimly tight

hauling me back before before
my mom and all
haunting me like kryptonite

until a sudden garden
brightens like a shimmering shore

which only hardens my hard-on

and I know that when a man longs
not knowing for what or why
this is what he's longing for

which only hardens my hard-on

women all fingers and cunning tongues
leaves aromatic swooning grasses
women all unguents or palpable gasses

only harden my hard-on

how they can be so many shapes
and all the universe is now this garden

and I can be this only one shape
like a wish come true I can't escape

Lois

It's being a woman or a writer
makes me so identify
with everybody in the news

including the corpses, I might tear
and open to the sky,
the buzzing buildings, hectic sidewalks and so lose

myself and shiver inside like water
with other places.
                    Watching superman fly
I know the currents and clouds that would confuse

me with their dizzy drift
are driven aside by his bullet resolve,

but watching I'm torn as a feather
falling then scattered in the updraught.

I, myself, and what I'm thinking of involve
and tangle together

as though today this new artist's
drawn me baffled by my features.
My face is like a vacant lot.

I'm cut off at the knees and wrists.
And robots and villains and alien creatures
go crowding into my silhouette.

Superman

I found an alien substance
always changing shape

that made me grow but also shrink
withered my powers with a glance

an alien being all agape
like a thing that's all a chink

and I read on its label
ADULT HUMAN FEMALE

and all I know is
I can punch my way though granite

Lois Lois
I am super-bodied and able

only this is where I fail
Lois Lois

my eyes could enter and seize
all the bodies on the planet

But wherever I go is
only ever Lois

whatever my eyes seize
only her aliases

Superman

I started to suspect the moon
is a fascinating woman and pale

and secretly her gravity
will undermine all men

will nightly conspire with earthly water
and every earthling daughter

always secretly on the pull

and so I wanted to transform the moon
into a solid dependable man

and hurtled up to do the Op
but hurtled *through* and couldn't stop

finding she was just a shimmery
image like a memory

and tried again and turned around
but found nowhere any solid ground

and then was pierced by a tremor
like fear for the first time of flight

nearing the source of the trouble
and bursting through her light

to find behind her glamour
only a desert of rubble

Lois

I was falling from the 50th floor
past all the flashing windows of Metropolis

like frames in which an action is cartooned.
Hard to remember who I was before

I fell from such height into such bliss:
that driven reporter, feisty, self-contained

who fell out of the sky into Superman's arms
like a baby swept up by my father.

We rise and hover and gaze down like a raptor
and see the ocean's urge to drown the shore

and the light that spurts from shuddering storms—
I've never, on a first date, gone further.

Cold light shifts across the rooftops of Manhattan,
flickers into strangeness the office where I work,

draws me, shivery, to its outlandish pattern.
Watching with the eyes of my alien captor

all I lived in day by day transforms:
the neon, the Coca-Cola sign, the *Walk* /

Don't Walk, I seldom looked up at the sky
and now I'm standing in it, like a metaphor

had gotten real that said that we could fly
if we believed enough in love's ecstasy—

I'm held up by my headspin like a helicopter.

Superman

A human swapped me, by a trick,
my body for his—

slack shoulders, creaky neck and knees,
slow dribble from his little dick.

I grow inside him, fill him up,
grow and grow and can't stop

bulging against his boundaries,
and this I'd never known before—

to feel myself to be a weight,
or walls without a door:

guilty this is one of many me's,
my disunited states—

I have no core,
I spread out like Los Angeles . . .

He talks like me, my parasite,
before this planet's eyes: the press, T.V.,

and wears my Clark Kent specs and suit.
But worse, *below* this,

wears my selves where I am most me,
unwrapping my Lois—

till she knows *this*
is not a superhero

by his smell . . .

then, like a frog kissed by a prince,
I'm woken by Lois from the spell.

But I am haunted ever since
we swapped our faces

by cravings that confined me:
corn dogs, tobacco, porn —

my strength sapped, my flight slowed, by traces
of a stranger that remind me

my self is torn
and I must drag this creep behind me

Lois

It's how he makes himself up—

his soaring away, his hurtling descent,
his boots, his pants, his vest, his cape.

Like making a person out of Lego
or writing yourself like your own author:

all action like a verb, no gap,
the opposite of hesitant Clark Kent;

no *or*, no *either*,
that *S* on his chest his own logo.

'Til this comic strip,
this trick by Lex Luthor

strands him undressed in this buzzing square
as though the world of human hurt

he intercepts to wear
on himself had turned him inside out

like a t-shirt
to show the dull reverse of his image.

It's too intimate,
seeing him so limp, so slack,

and turns me touchy as a bruise
staring into his damage

as though he opened a crack
that showed his whirring clockwork

and the dark secret of his bearded back.
I grow all tender to him like a bruise—

but worry as well this being weak
is just another brief disguise.

Superman

A superhero—and polite!

But how I want to burst free
hearing from all sides in the night
women's shouts of hurt ecstasy—
I taste their cries and touch their scent

provoking this surge in me
and my selves into argument.

I wash my car. I fix a leak.
I shine my shoes. I tie my tie.
Inside I'm hiding, like Clark Kent,
the power that grips me like a freak.

But how I want to burst free—defy
the army and the FBI,
and humans who are stupid and weak,
and spill across the 'papers:

carving graffiti in the sky,
King-Konging from the skyscrapers—

free as a public enemy
or one of mine, a wicked funster—
Mentalman or Sister Freeze,
Lex Luthor or Miss Rule.

But how I need to stay cool:
slot myself inside the boundaries,

grinning like a civil monster.

Superman

Off and on it's much too much,
being so powerful makes me sick:
X-ray vision, multitudinous touch
and even the tiniest most distant tang
in my chocolate mousse of garlic
screams on my tongue.

My supersenses open me wide
so all this alien planet
haunts me with its smells and noises
living where I ought to be inside:
each odour in turn, each cry—I *am* it,
swarming with everything, and no choices.

Lois's face is crawling with mites,
others are munching sperm in my bed.
What should be me is all of this instead,
scrawling the air with millions of flights
until I back away and sink my bulk
slack across the vast US of A and sulk

hearing the billion talkers demand
hearing their need I can't escape
until I wall up in my arctic bunker
wanting not to help or understand
but be alone and sleep inside my cape
like any other wanker

Sultry

The Café Bar of Rejection

Your body rejects the alien sown
inside your teenage being
whose rushes and plummets aren't your own
but you and *it* disagreeing.
Or maybe suddenly three unknown
keys are dangling from your keyring.
Love and loathing make you want to hide
and anger at your new Inside

and boredom at what adults are
and how you seep obsess and burn
out in the open in this café bar
whose staff as you approach will spurn
you like you're playing air guitar,
or squeezing your strange keys as if to turn
yourself into the one who opens
all the doors to where it all happens.

Saturday Night Revisited

I've always loved this city centre
and in my teens discovered
it's volatile
and at night can invent a
whole new identity
or at least a new style
as if the city uncovered
from inside itself another city.

Offices withdraw into shadow,
stores are empty except for mannequins,
the workers and shoppers go
and some come back to shop for spouses.
I'm divorced and back, it's eight years since
I used to come. Eight years ago
I'd not have frowned at the store windows,
their lounges in impossible houses

fixed where no-one feels at home,
where tramps slump and transients rent a
brief expensive room
and Banking and Insurance
riddle the centre
with the names of foreign parts.
This club again. The old feeling restarts
in me. I drink enough so the currents

on the dance-floor carry me away
where my youth's refashioned
by samples and mixes
so now is mingled with before
and the music dissolves the floor
I'm standing on, this floor of today
and opens stories downwards, partitioned
like *then* and *now* and *maybe*, unfixes

me like wishing or regret.
And then . . . I'm only polite
to a fat boy who shouts at me through his sweat
but I'm pulled into a fight
and bloody the nose in self-defence
of his girl, and break a nail and lose a lens.
I sit one-eyed and pissed at my table
loving it here where it's unstable

and dread the all-night buses
circling now through the darkening outskirts
on their tour of houses and spouses
chosen for life on such little basis,
and wish I could stay
here at this table
where it's all as changeable
as a store-window display

though my ears are numb and my eye hurts

as if I could uncover
from inside myself another person,
keep shopping for another version
of myself and another lover,
seat myself on a store-window settee
hand in hand with a mannequin,
keep swapping my identity
and all I've been.

Fully Explained

Where's it come from this obsession,
aimed so far from a fuck?
This love hardly at all a fleshy one:

not love more like aggression,
wanting to bite and scratch and suck.
Where's it come from this obsession?

Love as single-minded as a session
drinking clean around the clock
thinking it's just a fleshy one:

the self I thought was my possession
lost in always thinking *Fuck*:
where's it come from this obsession?—

turning the key in my damp ignition,
spinning my wheels although I'm stuck
on love hardly at all a fleshy one:

so I say to my shrink in our session
while he probes a hairpin in my lock,
repeating, *It's this big early Lack* . . .—

that's where it's come from, my obsession.

For in the Picture Sat a Plywood Gap

Smiling like moonlight over its brood
Of homes there sat a motherly, gigantic face.
I was a baby when I felt it fade
And cried at all the leftover space
And cried that there were only toys and food:
Perhaps it's always there, the sense something's ended—
Or did it start then, as my sight extended?

For now a crucial piece had been jigsawn
From the picture—like the loss of depth a wall
Confronts your look with when its mirror's gone,
Bringing you up sudden and short; for all
Dwindled in the mirror down to one.
Above the blocked hearth the wind's room muttered
And ached, as if the absence uttered.

For in the picture sat a plywood gap,
A perfect fit, its tenon precise, and its mortise—
A precious memento someone has let slip
Into a dustbin, causing fruitless sorties
To the dead harvest of the refuse tip—
Under the gulls scavenging at dusk
Picking through eggshell, empty tin, dry husk.

I entered the room searching but forgot
What for: it seemed the object of my search
Was there like an object in its name, and not.
Baffled I was tugged towards that place which,
When the plug's dislodged, tugs at your foot;
Which—as the negative in dreams (wrote Freud)
Does not exist—must be a place and not a void.

A place that's like the moment of transition
Where we always live and never settle;
Like moving house, the endless incompletion—
Nowhere to sit, stacked chairs and lost kettle—
Neither continuity nor supersession
In the waiting van, stirred dust or packed cases,
But both mingled differently in different places:

Enormous sky and ploughland flat as sea,
The white horizon riddled with a hole
By a dark figure shaped to take a key,
An explanation close. Or here, where I stroll
Watching cloud shadow massively
Rising; landscape, for no reason, a brief whole;
Cow pasture, beeches, flies hanging in the heat—
Only today these make me feel complete.

Undercurrents of Easter

Sleepless in her lounge two flights
below sea level, I remembered nets
and starfish on the club's floor,
rudders on its ceiling. Bleary headlights
undulated in her window through a flaw
spattered by a week's rain, and cars floated past
under the fish-bowl's surface upside down.
The dance-floor girls swam by the ottoman
she left me to—their lipstick ovals pursed
and widened, pursed and widened, miming, caught
in nets and jostled to a beat.
Moonlight in her mirror that raindrops dispersed
was like a chink of water bright with spawn—
faces in windows, lunes that germinate
in lit facets of pint glasses.

I'm threatened by water but immersed
in a bowl of air. A fat tide rises
fizzing with spume and curving with hips.
I think of her forbidden room as the dawn's
pullulating; at the roadsides, lips
wriggling in pavements tickling the wet
pavements pink; gardens
overgrown and dripping, grume fat
on their climbing, bushy awns;
enormous eggs in the brooding stores.
Oh let my hand grow and undo the flats
that are zipped up the middle with lit stairs!

Sultry

I'm thoroughly empty and dozing
and the drone of your vibrator

is a light aircraft circling
high on a thundery afternoon

where the parched view from its window
stretches almost

to where the sea rippling
is a troubled unreachable shimmer

Printed in the United Kingdom
by Lightning Source UK Ltd.
115740UKS00001B/136-162